Londinium: The History of the Ancient Roman City that Became London

By Charles River Editors

A statue of Trajan in front of the ruins of a Roman wall in London

About Charles River Editors

Charles River Editors provides superior editing and original writing services across the digital publishing industry, with the expertise to create digital content for publishers across a vast range of subject matter. In addition to providing original digital content for third party publishers, we also republish civilization's greatest literary works, bringing them to new generations of readers via ebooks.

Sign up here to receive updates about free books as we publish them, and visit Our Kindle Author Page to browse today's free promotions and our most recently published Kindle titles.

Introduction

John Winfield's picture of parts of the Roman wall in London

Londinium

The famous conqueror from the European continent came ashore with thousands of men, ready to set up a new kingdom in England. The Britons had resisted the amphibious invasion from the moment his forces landed, but he was able to push forward. In a large winter battle, the Britons' large army attacked the invaders but was eventually routed, and the conqueror was able to set up a new kingdom.

Over 1,100 years before William the Conqueror became the King of England after the Battle of Hastings, Julius Caesar came, saw, and conquered part of "Britannia," setting up a Roman province with a puppet king in 54 B.C. In the new province, the Romans eventually constructed a military outpost overlooking a bridge across the River Thames. The new outpost was named Londinium, and it covered just over two dozen acres.

For most of the past 1,000 years, London has been the most dominant city in the world, ruling over so much land that it was said the Sun never set on the British Empire. With the possible exception of Rome, no city has ever been more important or influential than London in human history. Thus, it was only fitting that it was the Romans who established London as a prominent city.

Londinium was initially little more than a small military outpost near the northern boundary of the Roman province of Britannia, but its access to the River Thames and the North Sea made it a valuable location for a port. During the middle of the first century A.D., the Romans conducted another invasion of the British Isles, after which Londinium began to grow rapidly. As the Romans stationed legions there to defend against the Britons, Londinium became a thriving international port, allowing trade with Rome and other cities across the empire.

By the 2nd century A.D., Londinium was a large Roman city, with tens of thousands of inhabitants using villas, palaces, a forum, temples, and baths. The Roman governor ruled from the city in a basilica that served as the seat of government. What was once a 30 acre outpost now spanned 300 acres and was home to nearly 15,000 people, including Roman soldiers, officials and foreign merchants. The Romans also built heavy defenses for the city, constructing several forts and the massive London Wall, parts of which are still scattered across the city today. Ancient Roman remains continue to dot London's landscape today, reminding everyone that almost a millennium before it became the home of royalty, London was already a center of power.

Londinium: The History of the Ancient Roman City that Became London analyzes the history of this influential Roman settlement. Along with pictures of important people, places, and events, you will learn about Londinium like never before, in no time at all.

Londinium: The History of the Ancient Roman City that Became London

About Charles River Editors

Introduction

Chapter 1: Roman Britain and the Founding of Londinium

Britain was a late addition to the Roman Empire. Being an island on the edge of the known world, it was a low priority for the conquering armies of Rome, and even when Julius Caesar first invaded the country 55 BCE and again the next year, many historians believe it was more of a propaganda campaign than a serious attempt at conquest. The first attack started late in the summer season and achieved little other than the claiming of hostages from two Celtic tribes, though the second attack was more determined, with a larger force and better knowledge of the terrain and enemy.

Andreas Wahra's picture of an ancient bust of Caesar

Julius Caesar faced hard fighting; by the time he got to the River Thames, which he found defended by a large force of Celts arrayed behind a wall of sharpened stakes. The Romans eventually deployed an armored war elephant that scared off the defenders, and after more fighting, Julius Caesar extracted tribute and hostages from several tribes. He then took his legions and sailed back to the European mainland, leaving a puppet king named Mandubracius in charge of the Trinovantes, one of the most powerful tribes.

For the next century, trade and diplomatic contact with the Britons increased, and Roman influence can be seen in Celtic imitations of Roman coins and Roman imports found at Celtic sites in Britain. Trade inevitably went both ways, as tin, hunting dogs, and slaves made their way south from the island. However, it wasn't until the reign of Claudius (ruled 41-54 CE) that a serious invasion was launched. In 43 CE, using infighting among the Britons as an excuse, Claudius sent four legions and an equal number of auxiliary troops, some 40,000 men in all, on a full-scale invasion. The force quickly took much of southeast England and pushed beyond the Thames. Arches in honor of Claudius in Rome, France, and Turkey all state that he "received the surrender of eleven kings of the Britons defeated without any loss, and first brought barbarian peoples across the Ocean into the dominion of the Roman people."

Marie-Lan Nguyen's picture of an ancient bust of Claudius

Over the next 40 years, successive emperors pushed further up the island and consolidated their gains by brutally suppressing revolts, including the uprising of Boudicca, queen of the Iceni, in 60-61 CE. The actual fighting was left to the provincial governors, the most famous of which was Gnaeus Julius Agricola, who took office in 78 and immediately launched an ambitious campaign of conquest. He suppressed an independence movement in Wales and then turned his sights north, marching deep into the Scottish Highlands before being recalled to Rome in 84.

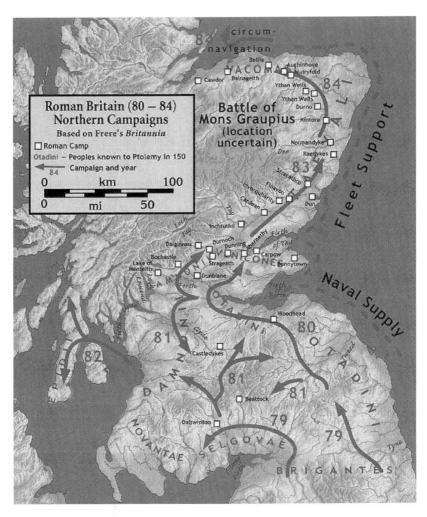

A map of Roman campaigns and conquests in Britain during the time of Agricola

Later governors did not continue his conquests. The Caledonians or *Caledonii*, as the Romans called the people of the Highlands, were fierce warriors defending a rugged landscape with little in the way of natural resources. This didn't give the Romans much of an incentive to launch a risky and costly campaign, and thus, the northern border of Britannia (Roman Britain) was settled roughly where Hadrian's Wall was later built. While there was no continuous defense, the border was more or less marked by a military road called the Stanegate, which connected Corbridge to Carlisle. Several forts were placed along its length, including Vindolanda, made famous for the discovery there of a cache of well-preserved letters dating to the Roman period. Treaties with local kings, not military might, secured the northern border at this time. These agreements weren't always reliable, however, and a more secure system of defense was eventually needed.

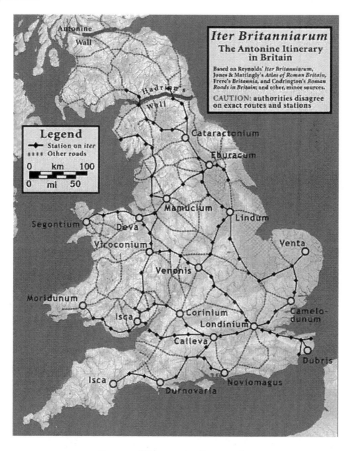

A map of Roman road networks

Picture of the ruins of a bathhouse at Vindolanda

In the meantime, development of the settled areas proceeded apace. By the reign of Hadrian, Britannia was a fully developed province of Rome. It is often thought that Roman Britain was a bleak, underdeveloped outpost, but this wasn't the case; by this time, Londinium was a flourishing provincial capital with the largest stadium north of the Alps, and well-built roads connected it to a series of smaller cities and continued all the way to the frontier. In the countryside were large farms and sumptuous villas decorated with fine mosaics and stocked with the best imports from the Empire.

It has been argued that Britain was developing its own towns in the Iron Age, immediately before the Roman invasion, and there were certainly some larger settlements as people gathered together in growing numbers, but these Iron Age settlements had little in common with what people in Europe at the time would think of as cities and towns. They used mostly the same construction materials and designs as villages, lacking the diversity and close packed living of an urban center. The Roman approach to towns was therefore something entirely new, which may have astounded, bewildered and even intimidated the locals. As time would tell, native Britons were not too intimidated to start using these new settlements, or to burn several (Londinium included) to the ground.

Unlike the planned cities the Romans deliberately founded in some parts of the country, Londinium emerged independently from the system of colonial rule and settlement. As a result, it was not founded near a large native settlement the Romans wanted to dominate, or in a position from which it could govern one of the provincial regions. Rather, it emerged at a transport intersection, growing through private endeavor until the authorities recognized its significance and chose to make use of this in governing the province.

Like many colonial Roman cities, Londinium was established in a raised position close to a river. The River Thames provided many of the things that a town needed, and of which Rome's urban planners were very aware; it was a source of water for drinking, cleaning and growing food, and it could also carry away sewage, a process now considered vital but which would often go neglected in British cities after the fall of Rome. Of course, it also provided a transport link in a time when travel was slow and often difficult. In antiquity, water transport was by far the easiest and most cost efficient way of transporting both bulk goods and people over long distances. Thus, a river terrace on the Thames' north bank and sand banks on the south side of the river provided ground on which to found the city.

For all of those reasons, the Thames proved instrumental in the rise of Londinium. As a transport link, it allowed both news and trade to flow in and out of the city. It was wide enough to carry a great deal of traffic, and Londinium soon developed long stretches of wharfs catering to this trade.

While this didn't make the city unique among settlements in Britain, its proximity to the continent did. It was a short haul from Europe to southeast England and so to the mouth of the Thames. With the easy journey from there upriver to London, it was the safest, most reliable way to bring goods into this growing imperial province. As a result, Londinium became Britain's central connection not just to the rest of the Empire but to its neighbors beyond the borders of Rome.

The ability to cross the Thames further cemented Londinium's position as a transport hub. Within years of the Roman invasion, a bridge had been built across the river, close to the location of the modern London Bridge. Between the key road connection this provided and the river connection of the Thames itself, it became an important center for travel and trade. Businessmen arrived to provide services to the soldiers and administrators serving the area, and soon a thriving city lay on what had previously been empty land. Even in the early days, this city was planned and organized by its residents, even possibly in part by foreign traders wanting a settlement in good order through which to work since Londinium was not an official colony. Growing to 330 acres, it was soon the largest city in Britain, a status it achieved shortly before being burned down in Boudica's native revolt.

Politics may also have played a part in Londinium's location and growth. Lying away from the regional centers and the power of local tribal elites, it was in neutral territory, which made it easier for traders from there to deal with all the different factions still existing within conquered Britain.

Such was Londinium's growth that it quickly attracted official attention. A garrison of troops was based in the city (initially in temporary forts while a more permanent base was built), the procurator quickly moved to the town, and the governor almost certainly did so as well. Thus, by the end of the 1st century B.C., Londinium was the de facto capital of the province of Britannia, if not the official capital. Public buildings were going up to serve the population and provide a sense of Roman civilization, and it was a major center of military, administrative and commercial activities. On a site that had been uninhabited only 60 years before, there now stood a city that would come to dominate England for the next 2,000 years.

Chapter 2: Boudica

Londinium faced one serious setback during the early years of its development, and that came during Boudica's revolt. The queen of the Iceni tribe, Boudica led a large uprising against Roman rule in 60-61A.D. Enraged by the terrible treatment she received from the Romans, and by Rome's annexation of the Iceni lands upon her husband's death, she gathered other tribes behind her and set out to destroy the invaders.

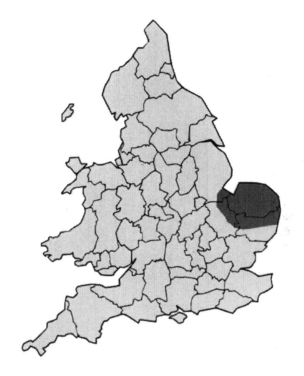

A map highlighting the Iceni lands

A. Brady's picture of the statue of Boudica near Westminster Pier in London

At first, the authorities were unable to prevent the advance of the Boudican revolt. Seeing that Londinium was in peril, they evacuated the city as part of a general withdrawal in the face of the approaching army, and this proved a wise move. When the Iceni reached Londinium, they pillaged and burned down the city, killing all inhabitants who had remained.

The Roman historian Tacitus, writing in the 1st century shortly after these events, wrote, "At first, he hesitated as to whether to stand and fight there. Eventually, his numerical inferiority— and the price only too clearly paid by the divisional commander's rashness—decided him to sacrifice the single city of Londinium to save the province as a whole. Unmoved by lamentations and appeals, Suetonius gave the signal for departure. The inhabitants were allowed to accompany him. But those who stayed because they were women, or old, or attached to the place, were slaughtered by the enemy...Alarmed by this disaster and by the fury of the province which he had goaded into war by his rapacity, the procurator Catus crossed over into Gaul. Suetonius, however, with wonderful resolution, marched amidst a hostile population to Londinium, which, though undistinguished by the name of a colony, was much frequented by a number of merchants and trading vessels. Uncertain whether he should choose it as a seat of war, as he looked round on his scanty force of soldiers, and remembered with what a serious warning the rashness of Petilius had been punished, he resolved to save the province at the cost of a single town. Nor did the tears and weeping of the people, as they implored his aid, deter him from giving the signal of departure and receiving into his army all who would go with him. Those who were chained to the spot by the weakness of their sex, or the infirmity of age, or the attractions of the place, were cut off by the enemy."

Boudica's revolt was eventually halted at the Battle of Watling Street. According to Tacitus, Suetonius told his men before the fight, "Ignore the racket made by these savages. There are more women than men in their ranks. They are not soldiers - they're not even properly equipped. We've beaten them before and when they see our weapons and feel our spirit, they'll crack. Stick together. Throw the javelins, then push forward: knock them down with your shields and finish them off with your swords. Forget about plunder. Just win and you'll have everything."

In the end, the rebels were suppressed in a fashion as brutal as their own assault, but the damage had been done; the thriving port growing on the banks of the Thames was left as a charred ruin and a dark streak in the historic dirt. Though this could have been the setback that obliterated Londinium, Boudica's revolt instead became essential in the city's development. One of three urban centers targeted by the rebels, it was rebuilt following the failure of the revolt. Before the revolt, Londinium had evolved in the manner of a frontier town, and it had lacked any defenses to protect it from the attack. Naturally, things changed in the aftermath of the revolt, as walls and ditches were constructed to defend Londinium and the city was rebuilt within them. The new procurator for the province, Gaius Julius Alpinus Classicianus, chose the city as his base of operations, and it seems likely that the governor was also based there. Buildings were put up by the government, and the governor may have had a palace within the city walls, though its identity has not been completely confirmed.

Picture of the ruins of a Roman bastion in Londinium

Once the city was rebuilt, the Thames, London's main thoroughfare throughout most of its history, lay to the south of the walled city of Londinium, which pressed against its north bank. To the south were marshes and the sand banks that rose up out of them even at high tide. At the time, the river was tidal at least as far as upstream as Londinium, rising and falling with the tide on the North Sea. The town's wharfs and buildings would have had to be constructed with this in mind, and it would have affected both transport and how easily water could be accessed at different times of day.

During the Roman Empire, the Thames was wider than it is now. Successive layers of embankments have encroached upon the river over the centuries, leaving what was once the riverbank now far inland, but in Roman times, it was a wider waterway that flowed south of the city, and whose ebb and flow was part of the rhythm of life.

Roman law, together with a disinterest by tribal elites in sharing their space with the invaders, prevented many villas from being built within five miles of a Romano-British town. For Londinium, this seems to have extended to 15-20 miles, though any law governing this and the reasons behind it have been lost over time. Perhaps the town was just so far from the interests of the traditional elites that they did not want to build nearby, while immigrants were more interested in living within the city. Whatever the causes, this meant that the city stood in splendid isolation, with all the significant buildings contained in a single place that could be covered by a day's walk.

Chapter 3: The Economy

The physical embodiment of the Roman economy, its coinage, was the same in Londinium as everywhere else in the empire. From the gold aureus down to the bronze quadrans, coins in early Roman Britain had their value defined by their size and the metal they were struck from. Most bore a portrait of the emperor on one side, or occasionally one of his family members, and on the other side there was typically an image of a god or the embodiment of a virtue. In this way, coins represented the principal pillars of Rome's strength: its political and military authority; its economic wealth; and the religion which bound society together.

There was coinage in Britain before the Romans, as Celtic tribes minted coins out of gold and silver. However, Roman coins quickly came to dominate, and Celtic currency eventually disappeared from circulation and played only a small role in the economic life of Londinium.

Though Roman gold coins existed in Londinium, they were not used for day-to-day exchanges, so they are usually found by archaeologists only in hoards. Daily business was conducted with the silver denarius and lesser coins, including fake denarii made by coating a copper core with silver, and which many people seem to have been able to distinguish from the real thing.

Over time, the coins were increasingly debased by mixing in other metals as the imperial authorities tried to make their precious metals stretch further. By the early 4th century A.D., few of the coins used in Londinium were worth anything like their supposed value, and everyone knew it. The citizens of the Roman Empire could tell good coinage from bad, and the face value of coins was increasingly dismissed.

Pictures of gold coins found in London

Pictures of silver coins found in London

The new gold solidus went some way to reforming this situation in a belated attempt to restore economic stability, and by that point, Britain was one of the few places where silver coins were regularly struck in preference to gold, which may reflect the fact that Britain was one of the poorer provinces of the Empire. Londinium was a wealthy city only by the standards of the surrounding territory, not those of cosmopolitan Rome, and the Empire was no longer trying to run a system based on both gold and silver, as the relative values of the two fluctuated. Instead, copper coins were used to represent a proportion of the value of a gold coin. Still, silver continued to play an important part in trade and business in Londinium.

The fact that coins were being struck in Londinium at all in this period was something of an aberration. Until the late 3rd century, coins had never been minted in Britain; they were previously imported from the continent, mostly from Rome but also from Arles, Lyons and Trier.

In 286, the Roman general Carausius, who had made a name for himself battling pirates in the seas around Britain, declared himself Emperor. Based in Britain, he founded a mint in Londinium to produce his own coinage, and even after his downfall in 293, the mint remained in official use and produced coins for this far-flung province of the empire. Central authority over coinage was eventually restored, and by 325 the Londinium mint's coinage was no longer considered official, though it continued to circulate alongside imperial coinage. After all, it was still precious metal, and it still bore the same symbols as imperial currency.

The citizens of Londinium paid taxes, along with other Britons, to support the administration governing the province and the troops guarding it. This included a poll tax and an inheritance tax on estates. As a major trade center, Londinium would also have had a lot of customs duties collected - taxes on goods moved from one district of the Empire to another - as well as sales taxes on specific transactions (such as the sale of slaves).

The burden of taxation increased over the centuries as Rome's income from conquering new territories fell and its expenditures on an increasingly complex governmental system grew. Taxes had to be paid in bullion, as the imperial government sought to regain the precious metals they had spent paying employees. As a result, taxpayers faced the additional burden of paying money changers' fees so that they could convert some of their wealth into bullion. This only added to the resentment felt over an increasingly burdensome system.

All manner of goods flowed through Londinium, including pottery, glass and amphorae of food transported from Gaul, Italy and beyond. Even before the Roman invasion, Britain's economy was based on exporting raw materials such as grain, animals and iron in exchange for manufactured goods from the continent. It seems likely that this pattern continued throughout the Roman occupation. Londinium would therefore have seen goods coming in from the more distant parts of the island and being bought up by merchants. The merchants would then take them away down the river and out across the North Sea to the rest of the Empire. Meanwhile, luxuries such as glassware and jewelry flowed in along with other manufactured items, to be bought primarily by the elite.

These imports included not just enduring luxuries but also perishable foodstuffs from across the empire and particularly the Mediterranean, and care was taken to preserve these once they arrived in the city. A special warehouse built in a pit near Londinium's docks was probably designed to help these foods last. In an age before modern refrigeration methods, preservation was a substantial undertaking in itself, and the warehouse is a sign of the lengths traders and customers would go to for these luxuries.

After the initial burst of intense activity in the 1st century, the quantity of imports through Londinium's docks gradually dropped. It was still a major trade center, but as trade and commerce became established elsewhere in the province and trade spread out from that single critical center, activity became a little less intense. This was increasingly notable from the 3rd century onward as changes in military life led to changes in the economy. The British garrisons were more and more made up of men born locally, and they were often the descendants of those who had settled in the area after their own military service. This meant that the army, a major market for foreign luxuries, was no longer as attached to the Mediterranean culture and diet. The troops were also increasingly paid in provisions gathered locally rather than in cash, and this meant that there was less money around to be spent on imports. Indeed, Londinium's decline as an economic powerhouse came along with Britain's gradual detachment from Rome, proof that its economic fate was tied to the Empire whose traders had founded it.

The center of trade in Londinium, as in any Roman town, was the forum, where merchants and shoppers bartered and exchanged goods in the open air, under the watchful eye of officials working in the nearby basilica. Warehouses built near the forum provided space for merchants to store large quantities of goods, making this the space to conduct large-scale transactions.

The forum was not the place for everyday shopping. For that, there were smaller businesses established along streets around Londinium. Narrow properties were built to make the best use of prime frontage on busy streets, where passersby could be drawn in. Shops, light industry catering to individual needs, and even eateries could thus reach their customers and be accessible to all.

Londinium was a center of production as well as of trade. There were all sorts of craftsmen and manufacturers working in the city, from potters providing everyday necessities to jewelers keeping the rich in style. The members of many professions were formed into guilds, banding together to protect their self-interest by maintaining standards and working together.

The most common manufactured goods were pottery, which were used for storage, kitchenware and eating. Even the dead made use of pottery, which the locals turned into grave goods and cremation containers. Though the army had its own potteries, it also bought ceramics from local manufacturers, helping the industry to develop.

Since pottery was such an essential of daily life, it was usually produced and used locally, and most was in the simple 'grey kitchenware' style. Londinium had small local producers, such as the Sugar Loaf Court potter who served a small neighborhood in the 1st century, but larger industries, such as that producing black burnished pottery in the Thames Estuary, also kept the city supplied.

Some pottery was traded over longer distances. Mortars were produced by specialist manufacturers and imported from elsewhere in Britain or the continent, and amphorae were imported along with the goods they contained, the luxury foods and wines that came from the Mediterranean. High quality goods such as Gaulish samian wares were brought in for the wealthy.

The next most important type of portable goods were metalwork. Much of the metal was recycled, consisting of old and broken items being melted down and recrafted to suit current needs, but Britain also had major sources of lead and iron, and the latter provided a ready source of new material for ironmongers. Furnaces were used to smelt the metal, with the smoke drifting out into the surrounding streets. Large manufacturing firms used slaves as staff, allowing them to produce large volumes of goods at low costs. Manufacturing buildings, then as now, would have been noisy, smelly places to live near.

As well as businesses, forts had their own workshops, and the garrison of Londinium would have been no exception. Armor, weapons, artillery parts and even nails for use in building work were manufactured to ensure that the needs of the military were always met. With its own core of craftsmen and manufacturers, the Roman army never made itself dependent on contracts or private producers; they were their own military-industrial complex.

Metal workers produced luxury items as well as practical ones. In the 1st century, there was a goldsmith close to the likely location of the governor's palace in Londinium.

Manufacturers also contributed to the construction of Londinium, producing bricks and tiles. At least one tile production facility existed in the city, making resources for residents and the surrounding area. These were not products that were shipped far (due to their bulky and fragile nature), so it made sense for the city to produce its own, just as villas apparently ran their own kilns during construction. Some tiles were distinctively marked, especially those used in chimney flues; they might be marked with the tiler's name, a manufacturing mark, or a decorative scene. That said, most tiles were plain, with criss-crossing strips that provided a better grip for the mortar.

The provision of plentiful water was absolutely essential to Roman life. There were obvious uses including drinking and cooking. The Romans were also famous for their bathing, and the water supply ensured that this was possible not only at the grand public baths but in some private homes.

Then there was industry. Whether a potter looking to mix their clay or a blacksmith cooling their iron, almost every craftsman and manufacturer needed water for some part of their work.

On top of this were the needs of the animals and plants living in or travelling through Londinium. As a major trade center, the city would have seen a constant stream of horses travelling through, whether ridden by messengers or hauling carts across the bridge and back and forth from the docks. Nor was Londinium a purely urban space of buildings and manmade constructs. Trees and crops were grown within its walls, and animals were kept by households. All of these flora and fauna needed water just as much as the human inhabitants. Thus, as in any Roman city, a steady water supply was required.

Though Londinium was built to make use of the River Thames for transport, much of its water supply came from other sources. Wells were dug, and by the 60s chain-driven bucket systems were drawing water at what is now Gresham Street. Iron links dragged wooden buckets up a timber lined well nearly twenty feet deep, powered by a large wooden wheel rotating at the top. This was a more effective method than simple wells for drawing up the vast quantities of water that were needed for the city's industries and public services.

This was soon replaced by one of the most iconic of Roman constructions - an aqueduct system. Bringing in water from outside the town, a system of pipes and sluices controlled the flow of water into tanks on pillars at street corners. Rather than filling the tanks and then stopping, the system kept a constant flow of water moving through, to ensure that the supply was fresh and the pressure on the system at a suitable level to keep it moving without breaking pipes or outlets.

A sewage system was used to carry waste water out of the city and into the river, though it may not have been a sewage system as we would recognize it today. Though impressive underground systems are known to have existed in York and Rome, in Londinium the waste may have been carried away as much by open ditches as by underground pipes. These ditches were not even built for the sole purpose of carrying away sewage - they also carried out the vital task of carrying away excess rainwater and preventing flooding.

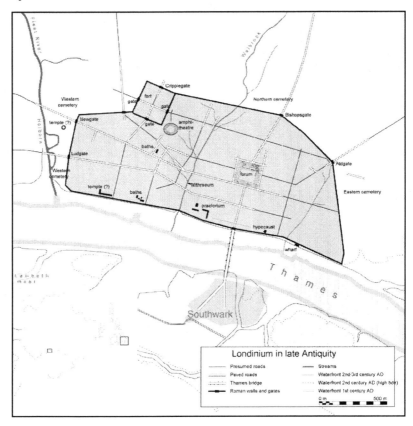

A map of the rebuilt Londinium, marking the known locations of the amphitheater, baths, temple, forts, and gates

Towns such as Londinium were vital to Roman society. Usually based on the example of Rome itself, they created a place of physical and therefore mental security that bound their residents together. Social and economic interdependence fostered a sense of a community, opportunity and shared identity. Natives as well as immigrants from across the Empire shared in a sense of being Roman that was tied to being part of a cosmopolitan urban minority.

The population of Londinium, like that of other Romano-British cities, was for a long time divided between natives and those who had immigrated from elsewhere in the Roman Empire.

Britons were seen as crude barbarians who needed to be governed by more educated, civilized men from other regions. They were excluded from positions of authority not only by this prejudice but by the property qualifications required to hold positions of authority in the Empire. There was a well established hierarchy with a clear career path among the politicians and administrators of Rome, and only those wealthy enough to be part of the senatorial upper class could be part of this. Thus, the relatively low wealth and status of natives kept them from rising upwards. In Londinium, as elsewhere in the province, there were ethnic, social and economic divisions between the rulers and the ruled, divisions which would only fade in the late days of the Empire.

Londinium's upper class included the governor of Britain, who was the emperor's personal representative in the region and probably resided in the city by the late 1st century B.C. Beneath him was the network of patronage on which Roman society was built, with those lower down the hierarchy dependent on their social and economic superiors. Important people such as the governor and wealthy businessmen had clerks and slaves serving them, but most people lived humble lives with their families.

At the bottom of the social heap were the slaves. Slavery was fundamental to Roman society and its economy. Slave labor saw the fields ploughed, water-wheels turned, and wealthy households served. During their working lives, slaves had no rights or officially recognized individual identity; they did as their owners told them or faced physical punishment. Chain gangs of troublesome slaves were used for hard labor and remained locked in those same chains in prison overnight. Once freed by grateful owners, the luckiest slaves could rise to respected positions in society. But for the most part theirs was a life of grueling misery.

Aside from government officials, the main group of immigrants to Londinium was the army. They provided bodyguards for the governor and fulfilled official roles such as policing the city. There are records of legionaries in Londinium from Gaul and Athens, and it is likely that immigrants came from as far afield as North Africa to govern and protect the city.

As a result, Londinium was probably the most ethnically and culturally diverse part of Britain, given its connections with the wider world and its large military and administrative population. Roman soldiers and officials were drawn from all over the Empire, and often stationed hundreds or thousands of miles from home. Merchants too probably came from all over the Empire, and particularly the neighboring province of Gaul, though there are less records for them than for the military. Slaves, though sometimes locally born, had to go wherever they were sold, and though we have little record of them as individuals, this was almost certainly another way in which the diverse population of the Roman Empire contributed to the variety that was Londinium.

Over time, this added to the mix of the city's permanently resident population. On finishing their military duty, soldiers often settled where they had been stationed, as in the case of Second Legion veteran Ulpius Silvanus, who became a resident of Londinium. Slaves were sometimes freed, and probably lacked the resources to return to their original homes. The civilian population was therefore a mix of locals, immigrants and descendants of the two.

A town's culture often has elements of all portions of society, from the youngest to the oldest and the highest to lowest. Some are better represented than others in what remains, but all are present. For example, Romano-British children had toys, including that most simple and universal of entertainments: ball games.

Of course, games were not just for children, especially when it came to Rome. Sports and games of a grander sort were a central pillar of Roman public life, and being a spectator in the crowd was part of the social glue that held citizens together. Games provided not only public entertainment but a part of religious festivals, and they contributed to the popularity of such occasions; after all, it was far more entertaining to watch men fight in tribute to the gods than to listen to a priest talk about religious duties and wave his arms around as he played with goat entrails.

Londinium had an amphitheatre for games, and it was built next to the fort in the northern part of the town. While no remains of a theatre have been found, these existed in many Roman towns, and it is likely that there was one somewhere in as important a city as Londinium. No evidence of a chariot-racing stadium remains either, and only one such building has been found anywhere in Britain, so there may not have been a race track. That said, chariot racing was clearly known of in Britain; chariot warfare was popular on the island before the Romans arrived, so this Roman sport would have suited the locals well. It certainly played a part in Romano-British culture, whether or not it took place in Londinium, and if the sport's supporters were anything like those on the continent, then they were a passionate group. Supporters of opposing chariot racing teams were known to fight fiercely in other parts of the Roman empire, mirroring the overwhelming and sometimes violent passion of modern soccer fans.

Similarly, gladiatorial fights were known about in Britain, but there is little evidence to indicate whether and where they took place. It seems likely that such games were held in the amphitheatre in Londinium, but historians can't answer that question yet with certainty.

What is clear is that large crowds gathered to watch sporting events at the town's custom built amphitheatre. Fans shared in the fervor common to modern sports crowds, riding the excitement of seeing their favorite competitors in action. This was the popular culture of the time, a thing that brought people together both in the crowd and in discussing the games afterwards.

There is stronger physical evidence for what is now considered higher culture: the physical arts. What is known of Romano-British art comes from the more enduring forms, primarily mosaics and carved stone. Sculptures in both stone and metal have been found, and statues such as a bronze figure of Hadrian were on display in Londinium. As well as publicly visible works, the interiors of houses were often decorated, with mosaic floors and painted walls. The rich in particular lived in spaces full of brightness and color.

A roman floor mosaic excavated in London

An ancient bust of Hadrian

Carole Raddato's picture of a white marble relief of Mithras killing a bull excavated in London

Public spaces and shared culture were very important to the Romans, and they extended beyond the cheering arena crowds. One new introduction to British culture was the bath house. Baths were a central part of life for those of influence in Rome and its provincial towns, and some went there almost every day to conduct business, gossip, and exchange news. It created an informal space in which patrons and clients could meet, and where even rivals might find themselves in close proximity.

The baths also provided an opportunity for leisure. With both hot and cold rooms in which to soak, as well as an exercise yard, they could create an escape from the cares of working life, even if that work sometimes followed bathers into the complex. They also introduced a standard of cleanliness and hygienic living, along with a change in the smell of those who bathed regularly, that was a new and exotic element among Londinium's urban culture.

For native Britons, baths never acquired the allure they did for the Romans, and though baths were built in Londinium in the 1st century, they were not as enduring a feature as some other buildings. Wear and tear caused by the hot, damp air added to the costs of fuelling them and providing a constant supply of clean water. For people living in a colder climate than Rome, and for whom these baths were a foreign import, baths continued to be viewed as an exotic luxury rather than one of life's essentials.

Roman culture, and in particular the Latin language, brought with it a level of literacy previously unknown in Britain. The very ordinary subjects people expressed in writing show that literacy was fairly widespread, not just used for administrative and official tasks. Many people in Londinium were probably still illiterate or able to achieve only the most basic words, but others could read and write fluently, as evidenced by the graffiti commonly found on shards of pottery. Just as in modern London, the walls of the city may have been have covered in the tags and small sketches of graffiti artists and those looking to assert their influence over public space.

Londinium was a busy city, with all the sounds and smells of commerce, industry and family life. The hammering of carpenters and masons; the cries of children and laughter of adults; the tramping of feet and the barking of dogs. With a large number of people packed into a small space, along with the horses that were used for all major overland transport, the smell would have been overwhelming by modern standards, even given the inhabitants' access to bath-houses.

Some people kept pets, including dogs and parrots. Some may even have had the Barbary apes that were kept by some households elsewhere in northern Europe. City life was not just for the humans.

Much of Londinium's food came from the surrounding regions, agricultural surpluses sold on to merchants or directly to the town's residents. Though some food was grown in the town and presumably in land used by residents beyond its walls, this would never have been enough to feed the large urban population. Though there are few records of such everyday activities as what ordinary people ate, the evidence we have points toward a diet based around grain in the form of barley and wheat. Beans were also important, as was beer, which in the days before purified water provided a safe way to stay hydrated. Meat included pork, venison, goose and chicken. Such high protein foods would have been much more common in the diets of the rich, the poor eating meat when they could.

The wealthy also benefited from the imported foods that poured through Londinium, at least in the first half of the Roman period. These included wine, olives, fish sauce and olive oil. They arrived from all over the Mediterranean world, particularly from Spain. Those who could afford them therefore had a more varied diet, though this was reduced as trade became more local in the third and fourth centuries.

The well off used silver tableware, though by the 4th century this was increasingly replaced by pewter. Made of tin and lead, this material was cheaper and so more cost effective for the rich, as well as more accessible for the less wealthy.

The average lifespan in Roman Britain is believed to have been somewhere in the 30s. In short, these people could expect to die at around the age when people now expect to enter the full maturity of working and family lives. This is not to say that some didn't live longer, as there are records of Romano-British citizens living into their 80s, and in one case to the ripe old age of 100. It is hard to tell just how exceptional these long-lived people were, but it is clear that, as in any era, those with better living standards could expect to live far longer than ordinary people.

The most basic deciders of health are diet and lifestyle, and this is evident among the remains of Roman Britain. The people of Londinium lived far more active lives than city dwellers in the modern world. Most of them walked everywhere, and even travel by horse or carriage was a more physically taxing activity than driving in a car or catching the subway are. Almost all forms of work involved considerable physical activity, and the only labor saving devices around the home were the slaves owned by the wealthy. Given all of this, the incidence of osteoperosis, a bone disease linked to lack of exercise, was far lower than it is now.

Though they weren't exposed to the huge amounts of refined sugar that fill modern manufactured foods, the teeth of the people of Londinium were still at more risk than those of their predecessors. Natural sugars in cereal crops, which became the basis of the Romano-British diet, led to a huge increase in dental caries and a smaller rise in dental abscesses. On the other hand, their diet also included some very healthy elements, including enough iron to avoid anaemia.

Large urban centers always provide hotbeds of disease, with the increased frequency of human contact vastly increasing the likelihood of transmission. The continent-spanning nature of the Roman Empire meant that these diseases could come from across half the world, brought by soldiers, traders and administrators, and unfamiliar disease would have increased the likelihood of death, as people's bodies were not well adjusted to deal with them.

Standards of hygiene in the city did not help, despite the best efforts of those running the city. There were public lavatories flushed with surplus water, a huge step up in sophistication from anything outside of the cities. But there was no home plumbing, and the inhabitants were not going to travel to the bath-house every time they needed to relieve themselves. Without an awareness of germs and how diseases spread, the inhabitants didn't know how important it was to keep sewage away from water sources, and the two often ended up close together, not least in the Thames, which had the job both of providing fresh water and of carrying away waste. Those using water from further downstream would have been at greater risk of infection.

Aside from the public toilets, another endeavor was also made to collect human waste, though it was one that probably did more harm than good where the spread of disease was concerned. Fullers placed jars at street corners for the public to urinate in. The content was then used in their business, as it was useful in removing the grease from wool. This act of recycling may have ensured that much urine was carried away, but it also meant that it was left sitting in open containers first.

In such conditions, it is hardly surprising that flies were rife in Roman cities. Evidence of fleas, lice and bed-bugs have also been found, a reminder of the tiny creatures with which people have always shared their cities, and which become particularly prevalent when many people live close together in unhygienic conditions.

The traces of disease are often hard to find, passing away with the remains of the sufferers. Stamps used by opticians to mark their treatments indicate that eye problems were common in north-west Europe. Gout was another common ailment. Even more serious diseases seem to have arrived in Britain with the Romans, as tuberculosis and leprosy reached the island.

Death in childbirth would have been frequent and infant mortality levels high. Such was the likelihood that an infant would die that they were not named and considered people for the first few months of their lives. The bodies of dead infants were sometimes buried within family homes so that their spirits could look after the house.

In shaping their own religious beliefs, the Romans had taken elements from Greek religion and fused them with local gods. The same pattern can be seen in Romano-British religious practice, as local Celtic traditions and those of the Romans were fused together in idiosyncratic ways. Similar gods from different sources were seen as the same or related, and became combined over time in the popular imagination, as in the cases of Minerva and Sulis. Roman ways of worship, as well as Roman myth, gave a new shape to local customs.

It is hard for us to get inside the minds of individual worshippers, and to see what part faith had in shaping outlooks. All we can do is speculate based on physical remains, but the substantial volume of these remains gives us much to work with.

Both pre-conquest Britain and the occupying Empire took the same fundamental approach to religion. A divine spirit could be recognized and worshipped in anything, from a province to a doornail. Natural places were among those most commonly associated with such spirits, though in urban environments the gods of important nexuses such as crossroads came into play. All could be sought for their support in times of need, and soothed to avoid their wrath during times of trouble.

Of the more powerful gods imported to Londinium, Jupiter was the most significant. As the head of the Roman pantheon he was also a symbol of political authority, and had official feast days on 3 January and the accession date of whichever emperor was currently on the throne. The imperial spirit or numen was worshipped along with Jupiter, and evidence from a temple at Greenwich shows the veneration of this divine spirit of the Empire in Londinium.

Jupiter's festival was far from the only official religious event in the Roman calendar.

Religious festivities were a way of marking the passage of time and asserting the dominance of Rome. Together with the physical buildings of temples, they made the imperial faith manifest, and made Roman religion part of regular life.

A temple precinct was built at Southwark around the turn of the first century, providing a religious center for Londinium. This included a shrine to Mars Camulos, combining a local deity with the Roman god of war. The bases of various statues and pillars on the site indicate that it may have been home to the worship of a diverse array of gods, in keeping with the Roman faith. A temple to Jupiter almost certainly existed somewhere in the city as well, and evidence has been found of its restoration in the third century, but its location and design remain unknown.

One of the most common forms of religious expression was the making of pacts with the gods. A worshipper would make sacrifices in expectation of receiving the god's favor in return, or vow to do works for the god if they gave the person what they wanted. The results are most easily identifiable in alter stones carved in fulfillment of such vows, but they could also be completed with smaller acts in keeping with the worshipper's wealth and status.

Sacrifices were important in pleasing the gods. Live animals and food or wine were the most common offerings, with the animal being killed and its entrails studied afterwards to see signs of the future. Sacrifices were most often made on special days, in keeping with the religious calendar, and preceded by some sort of procession, from grand public displays through the center of town to private processions around a house. Getting the details of religious ritual right was considered very important, and the minutiae had to be considered in every moment of the act.

There was no professional priesthood. Instead, all men could be expected to fulfill the role of priest from time to time, especially those of social and political power. Governors and city councilors would have adopted this position from time to time, making sure that public religious festivals were marked with suitable grandeur. It was one more way in which religion supported secular authority.

People wore their faith on their sleeves, sometimes literally. Jewelry inscribed with references to or depictions of gods was common, in particular rings. Worshippers also marked their faith within their homes, having household shrines to the gods. Statues of the deities were common, sometimes made from precious metal but more often from bronze. Though crafted in a Roman style they were not always created with a great level of skill, providing an affordable option for the masses to celebrate their faith.

One variation in the Roman way of worship was the existence of mystery cults. Coming out of the eastern provinces of the Empire, these became fashionable in certain parts of Roman society, providing a taste of the exotic in religion. Among the most famous was the cult of the Egyptian deity Isis, which had a temple in Londinium by the late first century. The cult of the Phrygian mother goddess Cybele was also present in the area.

Another prominent mystery cult, and one which was important in Londinium, was that of Mithras. Mithraism originated in Persia and offered the possibility of salvation through rebirth. It was an exclusively male cult, particularly popular among soldiers, and the temple in Londinium is the only one in Britain not linked to a fort. Because of its exclusivity and its connection with military power, Mithraism was a high status cult. The decorations from the temple in Londinium show that it was favored by the wealthy and the powerful, who had to be initiated and then proceed through layers of membership before learning the inner secrets of the cult. It therefore played a role much like Freemasonry would in a later era, binding together the city's elite in exclusive and highly ritualized activity, forging connections between influential men.

Mithraism met its end with the rise of Christianity in the fourth century. Christianity replaced it as the preferred religion of the governing elite, and without their membership the cult quickly vanished. Like other pagan faiths, it faced persecution and the destruction of its temples as the Christians rose in power, and some of the temple sculptures in Londinium were eventually buried to save them from this fate.

Christianity, which was just emerging in the east as the Romans founded Londinium, was initially just another exotic mystery cult like so many others. Evidence for it becoming significant in Britain is first apparent in the third century, and by the final century of Roman occupation it was growing in popularity.

Belief in the Christian god was in many cases not exclusive as it is today. Some may have come to believe only in the one god, adapting their existing ways of worshipping and reaching out to the divine in this new cause. Others combined him with their existing beliefs, adding him to the group of deities they prayed to. We cannot tell how widespread either practice was, as the evidence for each approach is the same - a mixture of Christian and pagan signs and artifacts.

There is no clear evidence for public churches during the Roman occupation, and it is likely that Christians in Londinium followed the same approach as many others throughout the Empire, gathering for services in each other's homes. This was still a largely private religion that excluded other faiths, at odds with the all-embracing nature of the classic Roman approach, in which all gods were accepted and praised together, new arrivals being absorbed into the eclectic mix.

But Roman religion itself was changing, with Constantine's adoption and legalization of Christianity. Though Constantine continued to combine Christianity with an acceptance of pagan worship, his influence made this once obscure cult into an essential part of the empire. After him, the atmosphere of toleration receded. In the 340s, pagan temples were banned within city boundaries and then beyond, encouraging the sort of destruction faced by the temple of Mithras.

Londinium, as an important city, became one of the centers for organized Christianity in Britain. The Bishop of Londinium was among those who attended the Council of Arles in 314, indicating that an organized professional priesthood now existed within the city. This separation of clergy from ordinary citizens was an important change. Councilors and other wealthy people were excluded from becoming members of the Christian clergy, to prevent them from using religious privileges to escape their fiscal, social and political responsibilities. Instead of being led by members of the community stepping out of their daily role, religion in Londinium was led by a new class of religious professionals.

Yet the immediate impact of this religious change in Britain would be short lived. By the latter half of the fourth century, divisions within the church combined with the crumbling empire to send people looking for other sources of divine protection. Paganism seems to have had a resurgence in Britain and its decaying capital of Londinium, even as the old structures fell away.

Chapter 5: Buildings

Adam B. Morgan's picture of a remnant of the Roman wall

Most of the buildings in Londinium were 1-2 stories, so they would have been invisible from outside the city, hidden behind the defensive walls. Though simple by modern standards, when compared to the huts of rural Britain, they were the height of sophistication. Built around timber frames, their panels were made of wattle and daub - a lattice of wooden strips coated in layers that combined mud, clay and straw. The wood gave the structure shape, while the mud layer filled gaps, providing insulation and shelter. Occasionally clay bricks were used instead. Either way, the buildings would have looked remarkably similar, as the outsides were cover in plaster and probably whitened using lime-wash. Later on, stone was used for some of the buildings, though they may again have been plastered, whitewashed and even painted. The taste for bare stone which people now associate with ancient buildings is a byproduct of the way they were found, not the way they stood at the time. In Roman Londinium, decorations brightened the walls.

Buildings were packed tightly in together, making the most of the space within the city's defenses, but this changed after a fire devastated Londinium in the first half of the 2nd century A.D. It was in the aftermath of this disaster that less flammable materials came into use and buildings became less densely packed, possibly due to general social and economic development, possibly as a result of local government intervention to prevent future fires. Great use was still made of the available space, commercial properties in particularly using tightly packed narrow fronts to cram businesses in where customers could see them. But the habit of packing buildings in as close as was physically possible was at least reduced.

Londinium shows signs of upper middle class housing in the early imperial period that are largely missing from other British cities. Normally many of the elite seem to have lived in the countryside, but in Londinium they chose to remain in the city. This may be a reflection of rules preventing them building villas conveniently close to town, or of the benefits of direct access to a vibrant economic and administrative center.

The houses of the wealthy had floors decorated with mosaics of small, colored tiles. This became more popular and readily available as the centuries progressed and Roman wealth and culture became more established in Britain.

The Romans were careful to lay towns out in an orderly, organized manner. The roads were straight for ease of navigation. They were not roads as we think of them today, with tarmac and asphalt covering the surface to ensure it stays smooth and firm. Rather, they were wide dirt tracks whose surfaces had to be periodically re-laid as they turned to mud or were made uneven by the steady progression of people, animals and carts. This relaying kept the streets usable, but it also had its downside, as it caused the road levels to rise over time. Home and shop owners may have found that doorsteps once well above street level eventually ended up below the surface of the road, letting even more dirt in.

Turning to dust in dry weather and mud in wet, these were streets that would have followed travelers into their houses at the end of the day. Worse than this was the other waste with which they were littered. Rubbish including rotting vegetation was made all the more unpleasant by the dung of the many animals living and working in the city. Not just dust but manure and refuse might cling to the feet of anyone travelling around the city. Like any dirt road, the streets would also have had plenty of weeds growing out of them, all the more so given the rich stew of dung and food scraps composting in that mud. The streets of Londinium probably looked more like those of a farm track than the roads of the modern city.

From early on, Londinium was surrounded on three sides by defensive walls and on the fourth side by the River Thames. A fort was incorporated into the northern walls, providing a base of operations for a permanent military garrison. But these were not the outer limits of the city. A bath-house and surrounding buildings recently discovered a mile east of the walls shows how the city expanded beyond these defenses, as has happened in the case of almost every walled city in history. The defenses therefore did not protect all of Londinium's buildings and inhabitants, but provided protection to its administrative and commercial core, a safe place to which residents could have retreated in the event of a threat, and a way for the authorities to retain control of the town in the event of difficulties.

The town walls were as much a statement of intent as they were physical defenses. They intimidated people coming to the town and allowed Rome to psychologically dominate the landscape, just as castles would allow lords to dominate in the Middle Ages.

One of the first significant additions to Londinium was the appearance of timber wharfs in the early 60s. Storehouses were built on both sides of the river to serve these docks. Private enterprise was the driver of Londinium's growth, but this does not mean that things happened chaotically. The streets were arranged in a regular pattern, with the land divided into rectangular plots called insulae. Major roads ran in from the north and the west through gates in the walls, intersecting at the forum in the center of town. This open space for people to meet and do business had been carefully placed so that anyone crossing the bridge into London from the south - one of the main reasons London even existed - would be channeled up a road directly toward the forum and the working heart of the city. Offices and shops lined three sides of the forum, with a large aisled hall called the basilica along the fourth side.

The basilica was the building of public business. A long hall consisting of a central nave with a lower aisle to either side, it was used for activities necessary to running the town, and built to meet that purpose. A raised dais at one end was used for official announcements and hearings. One of its flanking rooms was the curia, where town council meetings were held. Tax, census and legal records were also stored in the basilica, making it an archive of the city's past as well as a place in which its future was mapped out.

Londinium had the largest basilica in Britain, over 160 meters longs and perhaps as much as 15 meters high. By far the largest building in town, the basilica dominated in the same way that cathedrals would in later cities, towering above the homes and shops that sprawled around it. Lit by windows in the upper levels, it probably had a beamed ceiling which may have been plastered and painted to provide decoration.

A bronze sculpture of the head of the Emperor Hadrian, which was found in the Thames near London Bridge, probably once resided in the forum and basilica complex. Hadrian visited Londinium in the early second century, and the head is thought to have topped a statue of the Emperor, raised in the town's official hub to commemorate his visit.

Despite its grandeur and importance, the basilica did not survive the whole period of Roman occupation. This grand complex may never have been entirely completed to the designers' intentions, and it was demolished sometime around 300AD.

Another of the most important buildings, the principle bathhouse, lay in the southwest part of town. Resting against the slope of the city's gravel bank base, this overlooked the Thames, from which bathing water was drawn and to which it was ultimately returned. As one of the most important public buildings in the city, a center for both socializing and business, the bathhouse stood out among the smaller, more mundane buildings surrounding it, and saw a steady stream of customers going in and out. This was not the only bath-house in Londinium, or even the first, but it was the most substantial one and part of the improvement efforts of the early second century.

Bath-houses had to be heavily built, with walls thick enough both to keep in the heat and to support the upper structure, which may have included a beamed roof or may have been left open to the upper air. Hot air meant that the hot rooms of bath-houses often suffered from damage, due to the uneven distribution of heat and the expansion and contraction of walls that came with changing temperatures. They would have been subject to regular repair and reconstruction to prevent the whole edifice from falling down around its customers.

Londinium also contained that most infamous of Roman buildings, an amphitheatre. Home to gladiatorial combat and the other brutal sports favored by the ancient Romans, this building was located inside the town walls, near the south-east corner of the fort. It may have had military connections, as the close proximity of several British amphitheatres to military bases indicates an organizational connection. Alternatively, it may just have been considered wise to house the arena close to the soldiers who could if necessary bring the armed gladiators into line.

Initially build of wood and dirt, the amphitheatre was later built in stone to provide a more resilient and impressive structure. Like the basilica and the bath-house, it was a great symbol of Roman civilization, bringing as it did good order, clean living and what was then considered the height of entertainment. In a city of straight roads and square buildings, the amphitheatre stood out, a large ellipse with tall, curved walls of local stone. Entrances at each end let the entertainers in and out, while entrances along the sides allowed access for the excitable audience.

Local materials were used for most building, but not all. Dressed stone walls were made of Kentish rag, a hard grey limestone that was probably quarried from near Maidstone, making for a substantial but not epic journey. Looking further afield for materials, a monumental arch was built of Lincolnshire limestone, whose distinct color and texture would have made it stand out amid the local stone.

It would be a mistake to imagine Londinium as a purely man-made environment. Even in the most heavily constructed parts of the Roman Empire, the green shoots of nature found their place. Though little trace of them remains, it is likely that there were trees within the city walls, some grown deliberately in the centers of insulae as a source of fruit and medicine, others springing up of their own accord in waste ground. Weeds such as buttercup, chickweed, nettles and plantain were common, growing along the sides of streets, in wasteland, at the edges of buildings and in the drainage ditches that were essential to urban development in Britain's water-logged environment.

Dealing with these weeds would have been a major task in the summer. If left unchecked they could have over-run the city, and somebody would have had to deal with them. Without the chemicals now used to fight weeds, we don't know what was done to destroy them, but it would have been laborious work.

The variable quality of workmanship that went into Romano-British construction can be seen in the remains of wooden buildings. Though most of the wooden remains have rotted away over the centuries, enough have been found to demonstrate contrasting extremes. When necessary, careful planning and tightly fitted joins were used for precision building work. But in other cases, as at Londinium's busy wharfs, precision gave way to speed and sturdy construction, with crude timber frames joined together with large numbers of long iron nails.

Chapter 6: Governance

Despite its economic importance, Londinium did not have the official status of some other towns. At the top of the hierarchy were chartered towns called coloniae - Colchester, Lincoln, Gloucester and later York. Londinium was not one of these for most of its history, though it was eventually made a municipium, the tier below, and may have become a colonia in the fourth century.

Each town in the Roman Empire followed the same pattern of governance, an imitation of Rome itself. A hundred representatives of the local community formed the town senate or council, responsible for ensuring that the surrounding region was well run. To be on the council, citizens had to meet a standard giving them the status of decurion, a standard involving a certain level of propertied wealth. In a conquered region like Britain, this could cause difficulties, as land was taken from local leaders at the point of conquest. Some land therefore had to be given back to the natives, so that there was a propertied class capable of local leadership. Those on town councils also included military veterans who had been given land to settle in the colonies. This was therefore a body that exemplified the imperial Roman approach - an organization in which foreign military veterans and local people of influence met, the Romans becoming a little more like the natives, the natives becoming more Roman.

The council met in the curia, a room within the town's basilica. There they heard pleas and disputes presented by the people of Londinium, decided on the construction of public buildings and monuments to mark special occasions, and dealt with any other problems or questions that had arisen in the running of the town.

As in modern Britain, the town council had much control over what was built where and the standards that buildings had to meet. Any land not occupied by public buildings was allocated to the town's residents and their businesses, but this allocation was done by the council and under their rules. They seem to have used these powers to foster districts for commerce and manufacturing around the center, as in many towns since.

The whole town council of a hundred members did not have to be involved in every decision. Many of its duties were carried out through magistracies modeled on the Roman approach. These consisted of pairs of men given responsibilities for particular areas of life, the idea being that by splitting each post between two men they could avoid making any person too powerful, and reduce the influence of a corrupt individual.

The most senior magistrates were the duoviri iuricundo, who dealt with issues of local justice, organized religious festivals and took responsibility for running the council. As in Rome, religion was thus deeply intertwined with public life and government. The aediles dealt with public services and building maintenance, as well as entertainments in the town. Records compiled by the censitor were used by the quaestores to oversee the accounts, supervising local taxes and expenditure. And though we have no evidence for the existence of other lesser officials in British towns, they almost certainly existed in Londinium, as they did across the Roman Empire.

The holders of these offices were decided by elections. To stand for a position the candidate had to be at least 25 years old and meet the appropriate property qualification. The town was divided into wards, much as in modern elections, and ballots were held in each ward. To ensure honesty, men from other wards oversaw each election, having first taken an oath to behave honestly in this task. Though it was not representative democracy as we know it, the elections being run by and for a minority of the population, it at least gave local people a say in how they were governed. The holders of some posts may even have been rewarded with Roman citizenship at the end of their terms, providing an extra motive to cooperate with the imperial authorities and a way of further integrating Londinium's population into the power structures and culture of the Empire.

Despite this, few in Londinium seem to have reached the exalted heights that the conquered could attain in Roman society. There is no record of anyone from Britain, never mind the city of Londinium, reaching the senior senatorial or equestrian status. As these ranks relied on a person's wealth, it therefore seems that the Romano-British natives were unable to achieve either the financial or the political influence that many in other regions, including neighboring Gaul, achieved. A lack of inscriptions on public buildings further reinforces this impression. The government and the populations of foreign soldiers and veterans took responsibility for providing buildings and monuments that would sometimes have been funded by civilian natives in other parts of the Empire. This sign of wealth and status was not an option for the Romano-British.

While the native population accumulating in Londinium did play a part in their own governance, they remained excluded, whether by accident or design, from the highest levels of commercial and political authority.

The force of soldiers garrisoned in London did more than just protect the city from outside threats. They provided the manpower for most official activities, serving in administrative roles as well as providing skilled crafters and manufacturers for the legion and the government. When official buildings needed construction or repair, when roads needed laying or defenses constructing, this was often the work of the legionaries, and they had the skills to match. Architects and civil engineers, builders and laborers, manufacturers of tiles and bricks - the legion played a crucial role in maintaining the infrastructure of the city, and it is likely that they had a hand in planning its layout.

To support the needs of the town's administrators and officials, it would have contained a mansio. Though this building has not been identified within the remains of Londinium, one existed in every major Roman town, and they were a vital part of smooth imperial governance. The mansio worked like an inn where visitors on official business could stay, a place of rest while they worked in Londinium and a staging post on longer journeys that took them through the city. A large house with stables and a bathing facility, it ensured that officials and messengers could travel the Empire in relative safety and comfort.

While much evidence of Roman law exists, very little of it comes from Britain, and so it is hard to say with certainty what legal practices were applied. The same laws probably applied in the colonies across the empire, and possibly in the other major towns of Britain such as Londinium.

Wherever there are laws, there are also criminals, and their activity can tell scholars something about the state of law and order in Britain. Due to the activities of a Leicester glass-blower who melted down coins in search of their precious metal content, historians now know that this was illegal, and that the currency was protected by law. Evidence of extensive vandalism has also been found at a property in that city, including obscene graffiti, and it is likely that this age-old form of expression, still common on the walls of modern London, could be seen across those of ancient Londinium.

Petty theft was a problem, particularly from bath-houses, where the victims had their clothes off and their defenses down. The ability of the authorities to punish such criminals is unknown, but it is clear that the victims often felt a need to resort to other means of resolution. Curse tablets from other parts of Britain show people relying on supernatural rather than worldly authorities to see their goods returned and the perpetrators punished.

Soldiers were used to assert law and order, as well as to support the gathering of taxes. They were the face of law and order, making crime a potentially deadly venture.

Chapter 7: Decline

It is all too easy to slip into the habit of seeing Londinium as a stable place that remained much the same throughout the period of Roman occupation. In fact, over the centuries, the city inevitably faced changes.

In its early days, Londinium was not a border town but one behind the forward advance of the Roman armies and civilization, but it still saw extensive military activity, lying as it did on Britain's major transport and communication networks. After Boudica's revolt, armed forces probably remained in place for some time, protecting and rebuilding the ransacked city.

During the 1st and 2nd centuries A.D., Rome expanded and then consolidated its holdings in Britain. This was a period of growth for Londinium, with major public buildings being constructed. Much of the construction was initially done with clay or unbaked bricks, reducing the need to provide high quality stone, which had to be transported in from Kent.

The earthwork defenses thrown up around Londinium were replaced around the end of the 2nd century by stone fortifications. By this point, Londinium was important enough to be the first town to receive such treatment, as defenses were erected around all the important British towns over the following century. They were further extended along the riverside in the third and fourth centuries.

The growth of the defenses was more than matched by the growth of the town. Its population expanded, and with it the need for space to live and work in, the living now encroaching on the dead. Graveyards originally built outside the city ended up being built over, as Londinium continued to expand far beyond the limits of its walls and its orderly road system.

Political upheavals in the late 2nd century, followed by further disruption and massive inflation in the 3rd, reached out from the continent to affect Britain, but while these would have caused setbacks in the city's economic growth, they were not yet substantial. It continued to be a place of great importance in connecting the island with the mainland Empire, and with a sea between Britain and the political center of the empire, the violence of these upheavals seldom touched Britain's shores. Governors came and went, sometimes bringing more soldiers, sometimes taking them away to vie for power on the continent. Economic troubles meant that building work, a significant indicator of growth, slowed down, but for the people of Londinium life remained much the same. Military pressures on the edges of the empire, and even a revolt by a British-based general, did little to disrupt the city.

The beginning of the 4th century saw a period of prosperity, but one in which London's situation is unclear. Now the capital of two administrative areas - a newly created diocese and the province of Maxima Caesariensis - it was protected by the longest stretch of defensive walls in Britain. However, as other cities in the region grew, London saw little sign of a renewal in construction, with only a few monumental buildings put up near the southwest corner.

In fact, the 4th century seems to have been a period of decline for Londinium. Reliant on the troubled imperial economy, its importance came from being the gateway to a fringe province of an empire that was retreating toward its heartland. This is reflected in Londinium's physical environment. The forum and basilica had been demolished by around 300 A.D., and other public buildings were falling into a state of disrepair. Defenses continued to be improved, with bastions along the walls, but the riverside defenses were a blockage to the smooth running of the city's vital river trade. This resulted in, or perhaps was made possible by, the expansion of the city beyond its original limits. A bath-house and other buildings recently found a mile outside the walls at Shadwell indicate substantial activity down-river from the original docks. This area was still in use until the late fourth century, and indicates that, despite the stagnation at the heart of the city, commerce and its supporting activities continued to run through the city.

While there are few direct records of what people were thinking and feeling in the city, changes in the physical environment indicate a settlement that was no longer outward-looking and vibrant, with the world around it full of possibilities. Instead, Londinium had become a defensive place that viewed the outside world a threatening one from which the people needed protecting.

By the latter stages of the 4th century, Roman Britain was in serious decline. The empire was crumbling under internal and external pressures, and troops were gradually withdrawn. In 410, the Britons were officially told that they would have to fend for themselves. As local warlords came to prominence, Britain ceased to be a cohesive political unit, and local capitals sprang up. The age of the great capital of Londinium had come to an end, at least for the Romans.

Online Resources

Hadrian's Wall: The History and Construction of Ancient Rome's Most Famous Defensive Fortification by Charles River Editors

Other titles about Ancient Rome by Charles River Editors

Other titles about Britain by Charles River Editors

Bibliography

Billings, Malcolm (1994), London: a companion to its history and archaeology, ISBN 1-85626-153-0

Brigham, Trevor. 1998. "The Port of Roman London." In Roman London Recent Archeological Work, edited by B. Watson, 23–34. Michigan: Cushing–Malloy Inc. Paper read at a seminar held at The Museum of London, 16 November.

Hall, Jenny, and Ralph Merrifield. Roman London. London: HMSO Publications, 1986.

Haverfield, F. "Roman London." The Journal of Roman Studies 1 (1911): 141–72.

Inwood, Stephen. A History of London (1998) ISBN 0-333-67153-8

John Wacher: The Towns of Roman Britain, London/New York 1997, p. 88–111. ISBN 0-415-17041-9

Gordon Home: Roman London: A.D. 43–457 Illustrated with black and white plates of artifacts. diagrams and plans. Published by Eyre and Spottiswoode (London) in 1948 with no ISBN.

Milne, Gustav. The Port of Roman London. London: B.T. Batsford, 1985.

Made in the USA
Lexington, KY
10 May 2018